Learn to Code by Organizing Events: A C# Journey for Early Coders 1

Burak Turkman

ISBN: 9798860078819

DEDICATION

To my beautiful daughter, Anastasya, and my son, Ahmet, I send all my love.

CONTENTS

PREFACE

Are you an early coder who is older than 10 and ready to dive into the world of programming? Then this book is specifically crafted for you. We'll begin with the basics, ensuring you have a sturdy foundation upon which to build your skills. Whether you're interested in game development, creating apps, or even orchestrating your own events through code, this book serves as a stepping stone for your many adventures in the programming landscape.

We won't just throw jargon and code at you. Instead, we'll take you on a remarkable journey, showing you how programming principles can be applied in fun, practical ways. Imagine learning how to program by organizing a school event! That's right, this isn't your traditional programming book. It's a book that aims to instill in you not just the know-how but also the 'think-how'—the way coders approach problem-solving and task execution.

We'll explore everything from the fundamentals of C# to the principles of object-oriented programming. You'll learn how variables, data types, objects, classes, and loops all contribute to a programmer's toolkit. With each chapter, you'll gain the knowledge and confidence to tackle your own projects, making the transition from theory to practice seamless and enjoyable.

So gear up for an unforgettable expedition into the intriguing universe of programming. It's time to awaken the coder in you and discover the limitless horizons that await.

Let the journey begin!

Burak Turkman

CHAPTER SUMMARY

Chapter 1: Introduction to Programming Concepts

In the first chapter, we delve into the exciting world of programming, laying the groundwork for the rest of the journey. The chapter introduces the reader to key programming concepts such as variables, data types, and functions, in the context of organizing a school event.

Chapter 2: How to Work Within Constraints

This chapter demystifies the concept of object-oriented programming. We discuss objects and classes, using relatable examples like Participants, Tables, and Food items. We also go through the process of defining classes and creating objects, highlighting the usefulness of these tools in organizing information and activities for an event.

Chapter 3: Structured Data

Building on the concepts of Chapter 2, we delve into enumerators and their utility in storing and managing data. Through the lens of food choices at the event, we learn how enumerators help in representing a set of distinct items. We also introduce the concept of lists and how they provide a flexible way to manage collections of objects.

Chapter 4: Event Planning – Setting the Stage

With the basics covered, we begin to weave the threads together. In this chapter, we describe how we can use all the previously discussed concepts - classes, objects, lists, and enumerators - to define the structure of our event and lay the groundwork for execution. We design the Table and Participant classes and discuss how to manage lists of these objects to set up the event.

Chapter 5: Event Execution – Conducting the Symphony

In the final chapter, we bring it all together. We use the SchoolEvent class to orchestrate the school event, simulating real-life execution of an event. We discuss adding participants, arranging tables, playing music, and printing participant names. We also walk through a simple loop, illustrating the power of repetitive structures in programming.

INTRODUCTION

Hello young coders! Welcome to the fascinating world of programming. Imagine if you could command your computer to do whatever you wanted. Cool, right? Well, that's exactly what programming lets you do. It's like learning a secret language to chat with your computer. And in this book, "Learn to Code by Organizing Events: A C# Journey for Early Coders" we are going to teach you the basics of this secret language called C# (pronounced C-Sharp), one of the most widely used programming languages in the world.

I know some of you may be wondering: what can I do with programming? Well, the possibilities are endless. You can build video games, develop mobile apps, create websites, design animations, and so much more. But before you can do all that, you need to learn the basics first, just like learning to walk before you can run. That's what this book is all about.

In this book, we will take you on an exciting journey where you'll get to learn about how a program is structured, how we use different tools and methods to solve problems, and how all these pieces come together to make a computer do cool stuff. For example, we will explain how to organize a school event using programming concepts. Sounds fun, right?

Don't worry if you've never done any programming before. This book is designed to be super friendly for beginners. We'll explain everything step-by-step, and before you know it, you'll be understanding programming concepts like a pro.

Remember, you're not going to be writing any code just yet. Instead, you're going to be learning how a coder thinks and how they approach their tasks. And believe me, that's equally important. Once you get the hang of these concepts, actually writing code will be a piece of cake.

Now, get ready for a thrilling adventure into the world of programming. Welcome aboard, young coders. Let the journey begin!

1

INTRODUCTION TO PROGRAMMING CONCEPTS

In this chapter, we're going to learn how to think like a programmer. You know how in your everyday life you have routines and tasks to do? Programming is kind of like that. It's like solving a math problem or writing an essay. In math, you use numbers and symbols to solve problems, and to write an essay, you use letters and words. But knowing only the numbers or letters isn't enough if you don't know how to put them together in the right way to solve your math problem or write your essay. It's the same with programming. You need to know how to arrange the pieces to reach your goal. This chapter is called the "how-to" chapter. Let's start with some "how-to" tasks.

We'll start with things we all do almost every day. Let's talk about shopping.

Task 1: How do you get milk from the store? Here are the steps:

1. Put on your coat and shoes.
2. Walk or drive to the supermarket.
3. Find the dairy section.

4. Pick out the milk you want.

5. Pay for it at the checkout.

6. Walk or drive back home.

As you can see, to buy milk, you have to do certain steps in a certain order. Computers work in a similar way. They need to follow certain steps in a certain order to do what we ask of them.

Let's do another exercise:

Task 2: How do you watch Encanto? Can you write down all the steps? You can list as many steps as you like.

1. _____

2. _____

3. _____

4. _____

5. _____

Here's how I would do it:

1. Find the remote control.

2. Sit on the couch.

3. Turn on the TV.

4. Find the streaming channel that has Encanto.

5. Press the start button.

You might have different steps than I do to watch Encanto, and that's okay. We all have our own ways of doing things, but we still get the job done. The same is true for programming. Different programmers might have different methods, but they all solve problems. So it's okay to have your own way of coding. Just remember, there's no single "right" way to watch Encanto or to program!

Task 3: How do you translate a passage from Turkish to English? Can you list all the steps? You can put as many steps as you want.

1. _____

2. _____

3. _____

4. _____

5. _____

Here's how I would do it:

1. Get a computer or a dictionary.

2. Find the meanings of the Turkish words.

3. Write them down in English.

4. Arrange the words so they make sense in English.

5. Read it again to make sure it sounds right.

If you don't know any Turkish and there's no one around to help you, this is one way you could translate a Turkish passage to English. You might do it differently, and that's okay. There are many ways to solve a problem.

Now, let's think about computers. Can a computer understand Turkish? Can we teach it to understand Turkish? Think about this for a moment, considering what we just discussed. Write down your thoughts.

_____

_____

_____

_____

_____

Now, let's think this through. As someone who doesn't know Turkish, I needed a dictionary to translate the words into English. Similarly, computers need dictionaries, books, or libraries to understand and carry out our instructions. When they have their dictionary (in this case, a Turkish one), they can use that knowledge to translate from one language to another.

But what are these "libraries"? How are they made?

Software engineers create these libraries to teach computers what to do. For example, an engineer might prepare a list like this to teach the computer the meaning of certain words:

When you see this word	It means this in English
Merhaba	Hello
Kedi	Cat
Okul	School
iyi	Good

After being taught all these words, the computer knows what to give you when it sees the words you taught it. If it comes across a word it hasn't been taught, then it won't know what it means. That's why software engineers spend a lot of time developing these libraries. You can think of computers like students. If you teach them well, they can do anything!

Task 4: How would you solve this math problem: "(4+8+12-2) x 2"? Can you list all the steps? You can add as many steps as you want.

1. _____

2. _____

3. _____

4. _____

5. _____

Here's how I would do it:

1. Get a notebook and a pen or pencil.

2. Add up the numbers 4, 8, and 12 first.

3. Subtract 2 from the total of "4+8+12".

4. Multiply the number I got from step 3 by 2.

5. Write down the final answer and double-check to make sure I did everything right.

To solve this math problem, you need to know what the symbols "+" and "-" and "x" mean. Computers are taught these symbols and what to do when they see them, just like we saw in the Turkish to English translation example.

Computers start out not knowing anything, kind of like babies. But then we teach them things and give them libraries of information. After that, they can do all sorts of tasks. And guess what? You're going to be a teacher for your computer!

Now, it's your turn to create some "how-to" lists. Write out the steps for the following tasks, and then ask a grown-up to check your work and tell you how they would do these tasks. Remember, there are many ways to accomplish a task.

Task 5: How to find a plumber to fix your kitchen faucet? List all the steps.

1. _____

2. _____

3. _____

4. _____

5. _____

Task 6: How to order a pizza? List all the steps.

1. _____

2. _____

3. _____

4. _____

5. _____

Task 7: How to clean your room? List all the steps.

1. _____

2. _____

3. _____

4. _____

5. _____

Task 8: How to make a cake? List all the steps.

1. _____

2. _____

3. _____

4. _____

5. _____

Task 9: How to become a teacher? List all the steps.

1. _____
2. _____
3. _____
4. _____
5. _____

Task 10: How to jump higher? List all the steps.

1. _____
2. _____
3. _____
4. _____
5. _____

Task 11: How to plant a seed? List all the steps to accomplish this task.

1. _____
2. _____
3. _____
4. _____
5. _____

Task 12: How to organize a bookshelf? List all the steps to accomplish this task.

1. _____
2. _____
3. _____
4. _____
5. _____

Task 13: How to set up a board game? List all the steps to accomplish this task.

1. _____
2. _____
3. _____
4. _____
5. _____

In this chapter, we embarked on a journey to build a programming mindset. We learned that, like our daily tasks, programming is about following a sequence of steps to achieve a desired outcome. Just as we must put on our shoes before we leave the house to buy milk, computers must also follow steps in a specific order to complete tasks. This chapter was all about the "how-to" of things, and it helped us understand that there's a method to everything we do.

We also learned that computers, much like us, need to be taught how to do things. We compared this to learning a new language, such as translating Turkish into English. Computers need to be taught the meaning of symbols and words, or in programming terms, the "syntax." We explored this through examples of mathematics, where symbols like '+' and '-' have specific meanings. Once the computer learns these meanings, it can apply them to solve problems.

One of the important things we discussed was that there's no one correct way to do things. Every task can be accomplished in many ways. This is true for our everyday tasks and for programming as well. When we were solving tasks, we saw that even if two people do a task differently, they can still get the same result. This teaches us the power of creativity and individual thinking in problem-solving, both in our daily lives and in programming.

This chapter was all about laying the groundwork. The steps we take in our daily tasks are like the lines of code that tell a computer what to do. Just like you are getting ready to go shopping or to watch a movie, you're also getting ready to tell a computer what to do when you're programming. It's all about preparing, taking one step at a time, and making sure everything is in order.

So, in this chapter, we learned how to think step-by-step and why it's so important. We learned how to break big tasks down into smaller ones. This is a vital skill in programming, and it's also really useful in daily life.

As we wrap up this chapter, remember that you're on your way to becoming a computer's teacher! You're going to learn to give it detailed, step-by-step instructions to accomplish tasks, just like the tasks we broke down today. Keep practicing, keep thinking about the steps you take every day, and you'll be a pro at programming in no time!

Keep this knowledge with you as we move forward because these are the fundamental building blocks of programming. The next chapters are going to build on this, as we dive deeper into the world of coding. So stay tuned, stay curious, and let's keep learning!

Fun Fact

The first computer weighted more than 54.000 pounds

The Electronic Numerical Integrator
and Computer, commonly known as
ENIAC, was the first general-
purpose digital computer that was
programmable and electronic. It was
constructed by the United States
during World War II.

Fun Fact Activity

Create a fun fact for year of 2040

Imagine you're in the year 2040 and think about what could be considered a "fun fact" during that time. Create your own fun fact for the year 2040! Include a title, content and drawing.

Fun Fact

2

HOW TO WORK WITHIN CONSTRAINTS

In our last chapter, we explored how there are many ways to complete a task, and that everyone might have a slightly different approach. It was like being given the freedom to create a painting however you wanted. But imagine now that you're given a coloring book. There are lines and shapes already on the paper, and your job is to fill in the colors. It's a bit different, right? In this chapter, we're going to learn how to work within certain boundaries or rules. These are often called constraints.

Just as we have rules in school, or in games, or even at home, there are also rules when programming. We talked a bit in the last chapter about how computers are taught to understand certain languages, like Java or Python, and follow certain instructions. These languages were created by software engineers who thought very carefully about the best ways to tell a computer what to do. Now, it's up to us to learn how to use these languages to give our own instructions to the computer.

When we were thinking about our tasks in the last chapter, we were kind of like inventors, coming up with our own way of doing things. Now, we're going to be a bit more like detectives. We have a specific set of tools, or clues, that we can use, and our job is to figure out how to use them to solve the task at hand.

So, in this chapter, we're going to start learning how to work within the constraints of the programming languages that we're given. We're going to be like artists working with a coloring book, or detectives solving a mystery. It's a new challenge, but I know you're up to it! Let's dive in and start putting the pieces together.

Task 1: How to wash a car? Choose from the provided materials or scenarios and put them in a logical order to complete the task.

Given: Flowers, brush, sunglasses, hose, car, mailbox, coffee, towels, TV, water, soap, washing area

Complete the task using only the materials listed above.

1._____
2._____
3._____
4._____
5._____

Here is how I would approach it:

1. Select the car

2. Move the car to the washing area

3. Utilize the hose to wet the car

4. Use the brush, soap, and water to scrub the car clean

5. Dry the car using towels

Remember, your approach might be slightly different from mine. You could have considered the possibility of a sunny day, so you chose to wear sunglasses. Or you might have decided that it wasn't necessary to move the car to a washing area and washing the car in front of your house would be sufficient. What matters is that we both used only what was given to us and completed the task, albeit with variations.

In the realm of software engineering, when a programming language or a library is developed, specific tools, methods, and ways of accomplishing tasks are defined. Just like in the dictionary example we used earlier. Hence, to learn programming, it's crucial to understand how a language is constructed and what resources (tools, libraries, methods) are available to you. The more familiar you become with the language's structure and tools provided, the easier programming will be.

Let's move on to more exercises to practice this concept.

Task 2: How to pack a lunch? Choose from the given materials or scenarios and order them logically to accomplish the task.

Given: Refrigerator, sausage, cookies, backpack, lunch box, apple, water bottle, book, TV, cheese, school bus, pencil

Complete the task by only using the materials provided above.

1._____

2._____

3._____

4._____

5._____

Here's how I would do it:

1. Open the refrigerator

2. Take out sausage, cheese, and an apple

3. Put sausage and cheese into the lunch box

4. Put the apple and cookies into the lunch box

5. Place the lunch box and water bottle into the backpack

Again, your steps might look a little different from mine. Maybe you decided you wanted to take your lunch box separate from your backpack, or perhaps you thought that watching TV while packing your lunch would be more fun. As long as we only use what's provided and our steps make sense, there's still room for individuality even within constraints!

Like packing a lunch with a certain set of items, programming languages have certain structures and tools they offer us to use. For example, the Python language has tools (often called functions) for doing math, creating lists, or writing text. Knowing what tools are available and how to use them properly is a big part of learning a new language, just like how you learned to make lunch with what was in the fridge!

Let's keep practicing with some more tasks.

Task 3: How to bake a cake? Choose from the items listed and put them in the right order to make a delicious cake.

You have: Flour, brush, eggs, air-fryer, sand, tomatoes, coffee, cacao, phone, water, internet, cinnamon, parchment paper, yoghurt, oil

1._____
2._____
3._____
4._____
5._____

Here's one way to do it:

1. Grab your phone and use the internet to find a cake recipe that matches the ingredients you have.

2. Place some parchment paper in a makeshift mould (maybe you could use the sand and eggs to form a shape).

3. Combine the flour, eggs, yoghurt, water, and oil in the mould.

4. Put your cake-to-be in the air-fryer.

5. Use your phone as a timer to make sure the cake doesn't overcook.

Isn't it fascinating how we can get creative when we're limited to specific items? You might've thought of a completely different approach, but that's okay! The point is, we both ended up baking a cake, despite our different methods.

Just like baking a cake with the tools we have, programming is also about using the given tools and libraries to create something useful. Remember, the order in which you do things is crucial. Just imagine what would happen if you put the flour in the air-fryer before mixing it with the other ingredients!

Now let's put your skills to the test! Try the following tasks and don't hesitate to ask your family or friends for feedback. Ask them how they would approach the tasks and compare your methods. You might be surprised by the different ways you can accomplish the same task.

Task 4: How to order some flowers without leaving your house? You have these items: a map, refrigerator, florist magnet, credit card, phone (without internet), coke, bird, paper, bees, honey

Can you come up with a step-by-step guide to accomplish the task?

1._____

2._____

3._____

4._____

5._____

Task 5: How to teach tic tac toe to a friend without talking or writing? You have these items: chalk, cloud pictures, a silver medal, nail clipper, ice cubes, bird seeds, seats, black board

Can you figure out a way to do it?

1._____

2._____

3._____

4._____

5._____

Task 6: How to send a 'mail' without internet? You have these items: light fixtures, garden hose, flash drive, computer with a word processing app, address book, envelopes, cereal, mailbox, calendar, stamps

Could you make it work with these tools?

1._____

2._____

3._____

4._____

5._____

Task 7: How to keep produce cool without a fridge? You have a house with a garden, birds, bugs, clippers, shovel, bags, water, pipes, sticks, tape, electricity, sunglasses, a fan, a hamster, and a treadmill

What are the steps to make this happen?

1._____

2._____

3._____

4._____

5._____

These activities will encourage you to think outside of the box and find creative solutions, much like a programmer would do when faced with limitations. Remember, there's no single correct way to complete these tasks, as long as you use the items provided and accomplish the task at hand!

Task 8: How to build a fire without a lighter or matches? You have: dog food, hay, chicken, eggs, eyeglasses, water, newspaper, clock, flowers, sticks, sun, fan, sandwich, seat, radio, batteries, ice cream, copper, wires

What steps would you take?

1._____
2._____
3._____
4._____
5._____

Task 9 How to jump twice as high as you can now? You have these items: compass, magnets, spaceship, springs, grass, screwdriver and screws, backpack, school bus, lemon, vacuum cleaner, calendar, a computer with internet connection

What would your plan be?

1._____
2._____
3._____
4._____
5._____

Task 10: How to clean oceans? You have: sunflowers, life vests, floaties, baskets, brushes, phone, computer with internet, sunglasses, umbrellas, sticks, ladders, plastic covers, bags

How would you make this happen?

1._____
2._____
3._____
4._____
5._____

Task 11: How to take your cat to Disneyland? Here are some tools you can use: a boat, seat belt, empty paint bucket, scissors, bicycle, nails, rocks, lemon, freezer, table, cat, water, camera, a device with social media and internet access, headphones, food

What steps would you take?

1._____
2._____
3._____
4._____
5._____

Remember, being a programmer is like being a problem solver. You need to look at what tools and resources you have, and then figure out the best way to use them to solve your problem or complete your task. And, just like with these tasks, there's often more than one solution, and no solution is perfect. So keep thinking, keep trying, and keep learning!

Chapter 2 of our journey into the world of programming has been a thrilling adventure. We have explored problem-solving in a new and exciting way, using everyday objects and scenarios. Just like real programmers, we've had to find unique and creative solutions with limited resources, illustrating how coding isn't all that different from everyday problem-solving.

Our exploration began with a curious task of baking a cake with an unusual set of ingredients and tools. This exercise showed us that programming, like baking, requires careful planning and ordering of steps to achieve a successful outcome. We also discovered the importance of using available resources effectively, a lesson that's very much applicable to programming where we often have to work with existing libraries and functions.

We delved further into more challenges that tested our creativity, from ordering flowers with a credit card and a phone, to figuring out how to teach a game without speaking or writing, and even devising a way to send an email without an internet connection! Every challenge was a unique puzzle, just as every coding problem is. We learned to think outside the box and to apply logic and creativity to solve problems.

The task of keeping produce cold without a refrigerator demonstrated the importance of improvisation. In programming, we might not always have the perfect tools at our disposal, and it's in these moments that our problem-solving skills truly shine.

Towards the end, we grappled with bigger tasks like cleaning oceans, taking a cat to Disneyland, and jumping twice as high! These larger tasks helped us understand the scope of what programming can achieve, reinforcing the idea that coding is a powerful tool that can bring about significant changes in the real world.

In conclusion, Chapter 2 has been all about developing our problem-solving skills and applying them to various scenarios, drawing parallels with programming. The world of coding is vast and complex, but it's also filled with endless possibilities for creativity and innovation. Each task we completed was a step towards becoming better programmers.

We have seen how the mindset of a programmer isn't so different from that of an inventive child or a resourceful adult. The curiosity, creativity, and logical thinking we apply in everyday life are the same skills that make a good programmer. As we continue our journey, always remember to embrace challenges, think outside the box, and never stop learning. The world of programming is as expansive as our imagination and our willingness to explore.

Fun Fact

The first computer mouse was made of wood

Douglas Engelbart aimed to improve the world through computers and invented the first mouse in 1964, using a pine block, a circuit board, and two metal wheels.

Fun Fact Activity

Create a fun fact for year of 2050

Imagine you're in the year 2050 and think about what could be considered a "fun fact" during that time. Create your own fun fact for the year 2040! Include a title, content and drawing.

Fun Fact

3

STRUCTURED DATA

In our everyday life, we follow certain dialogue patterns to communicate with others. For instance, when we say, "Hello, Ahmet," this is a greeting used to start a conversation or simply show that we care about the other person. When you ask, "How old are you, Anastasya?", this is a question. You're providing an input and expecting an output.

We interact with computers much the same way we communicate with people. We provide a stimulus and expect a response. This is how we go about our daily lives and, therefore, we program computers to mimic the behaviors we exhibit daily.

Let's do some activities to understand what an input-output relationship is and how we order them.

Task 1: Arrange the following statements in order to form a coherent conversation:

1. At 9:00 p.m.
2. Have you ever seen the new Avatar movie?
3. Do you like 3D effects in movies?
4. I'm looking for a movie to watch with my parents.

5. Hi Anastasya, what are you doing?

6. Sounds cool.

7. It's going to be on tv tonight.

8. Yes, I do.

Write down your ordered list here:

_____, _____, _____, _____, _____, _____, _____, _____

When you look at the list above, you see some random statements not listed in an order that makes sense as a whole. You need to read each one to see the big picture and analyze the logic to arrange them in a way that makes sense to us.

We approach computers the same way we navigate our daily interactions with others. Software engineers have prepared many different options, methods, or functions for us to choose from. These methods are like the list you saw above. Instead of randomly invoking each item from the list, you need to follow a logical order to make use of these existing functions. Similarly, when you create your own functions, you won't call them randomly. You'll need to present them to users in a meaningful way so that successful interaction between a human and a computer can take place.

When we began this chapter, we noted that some of the statements we use in our daily life don't require a response from the other person. For example, greeting statements like saying hi to your friend. You're not asking a question, just acknowledging your friend. Let's examine this concept in the world of programming with our first few lines of code:

```
public void SayHello()
{
        Console.WriteLine("Hello, My Friend!!!");
}
```

As soon as you see the words "Hello, My Friend!!!" in the code block, you understand what this code block is trying to do. However, you might also start wondering about all the extra symbols and characters around the "Hello, My Friend!!!" statement. Let's dissect them together and understand what all these symbols and characters are for.

Let's start with the word "public" in the code block. In real life, you know that not everyone should know your secrets or that you shouldn't share some sensitive information with strangers. Possession of such crucial, sometimes confidential, information might harm you. Let's imagine you and your classmates are preparing for a science competition, and you have a brilliant idea to win the contest. You and your classmates are collecting all kinds of data and developing various procedures to carry out this exciting science project. As you know, this project is private to your classroom. Other classes or schools shouldn't know about the specifics of this project. To safeguard this valuable information, you and your classmates take certain precautions. One of them is not discussing the project in public. Another could be securing any kind of documentation or data so others can't access it.

However, this doesn't mean that you won't communicate with students from other classrooms or schools. You can greet everyone. Greeting someone doesn't require any protection.

When you look at the code snippet above, you'll notice an access modifier "public." In the world of programming, we call them "access modifiers." It determines who can access a specific method or variable or a class comprising various variables and methods.

However, if we're discussing the science project, it shouldn't be public. Any information related to the science project should be private to your own classroom. Otherwise, your idea could be stolen, and other groups could create something similar.

```
private void PrintScienceProjectPlan()
{
    Console.WriteLine("Anastasya uses a laser to tease the dog");
    Console.WriteLine("Dog starts running and sweating from his tongue");
    Console.WriteLine("Ahmet collects the dog sweat from his tongue using a spoon");
    Console.WriteLine("Pouring the dog sweat on an injured plant promotes its healing");
}
```

The access modifier we used in the code snippet above changed to "private". Since it's your class's secret science project idea and others shouldn't know about it, we made it "private". Individuals outside your class shouldn't have access to this secret plan.

Yes, using the "private" access modifier helps you to protect your methods, variables, and data from outsiders. We can make our methods, variables, and classes private. I realize we haven't discussed variables and classes yet, but for now, it's enough to know that these terms exist in programming.

Now it's your turn to decide whether the following methods should be public or private. Write "public" or "private" for the following functions.

1. _____ void SendMoneyFromMyAccount()

2. _____ void SayGoodNight()

3. _____ string BringMySecret()

4. _____ void AskForHelp()

5. _____ int ReturnCurrentYear()

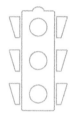

I'd like you to understand one more access modifier for now - "internal". Yes, it's neither public nor private. It's in between - "internal". Let's say your school has limited resources, and different classrooms share these resources. Suppose there's only one laser pointer in your school, and you have to reserve the laser pointer from your science teacher for your science project. Your science teacher creates a method that shows who can use the laser pointer during scheduled hours. All the classrooms in your school can see this schedule because they share the same resource. However, other schools don't need to know which classroom in your school is using this laser pointer. You don't need to share this information with other schools. They might also get curious and want to learn what you're doing with the laser pointer. Therefore, we are hiding this schedule from those who are not in our school. They don't need to know anything about your school's resources, who's using them, or when they are being used.

Your science teacher prepared the following function to print laser pointer reservations.

```
internal void PrintLaserPointerReservations()
{
    Console.WriteLine("Classroom: 4-A, Monday from 9:00-12:00");
    Console.WriteLine("Classroom: 4-B, Monday from 12:00-3:00");
    Console.WriteLine("Classroom: 4-C, Tuesday from 9:00-12:00");
    Console.WriteLine("Classroom: 4-D, Tuesday from 12:00-3:00");
}
```

In this code snippet, we used the "internal" access modifier. This means that only students within the same school can have access to this reservation list. Other schools will not know about this. Different classes in your school can check the schedule and get the laser pointer from your science teacher.

To summarize the three access modifiers we learned in this chapter:

Public: Open to everyone. Your class, other classrooms, and other schools can access the data.

Internal: Only classrooms or students in your school can have access.

Private: It's private to your class. Only your class can access the data.

Let's move on to the other mystery word, "void". You've likely come across this term before. For example, our parents write "void" on checks to render them invalid. There will be no money exchanged if someone takes that check to a bank and requests money. There is no return in that case.

In programming, when we write functions, we determine their return types. Some of them do not return a value but perform tasks we require, some return numbers, others return words, and others return true or false responses. Some of these magical return types include:

- Void
- String
- Integer
- Boolean

Don't fret about these terms or the meaning of return type. We will review each one and provide plenty of examples to understand them.

Suppose you plan to invite your friends to your birthday party, and your mother has requested an estimate of the total number of guests expected to attend. You decided to send an invitation and asked for an RSVP from them. If they are going to attend the party, you asked them to send a text message saying "Yes"; if not, the message should say "No".

```
public bool IsAttending(string answer)
{
        if (answer.Equals("Yes"))
        {
                return true;
        }
        else
        {
                return false;
        }
}
```

The code snippet above introduces some new elements and terms we hadn't seen before. For instance, between parentheses, we see "string answer". Also, we see "if" and "else" statements and the "return" keyword.

If you read it like plain English, you understand the big picture without deciphering the programming jargon. Essentially, if the answer from our friends is "Yes", the "IsAttending" function returns true for our friend's attendance response. Otherwise, it returns false.

"True" and "false" are the only values we can have when we use a boolean. In the function above, we specified the kind of answer we want by designating "bool" as our return type. When you type "bool" as your return type, the function must return either "true" or "false".

If you want a number as a response instead of "true" or "false" answers, you need to change your return type to integer. For example, if you want to learn someone's age, you wouldn't want an answer that returns true or false, unless you are playing a guessing game with your friend.

```
public int AgeCalculator(int yearOfBirth, int currentYear)
{
    return currentYear - yearOfBirth;
}
```

In the example above, we changed the return type to "int". This means that we want a number as a return. When you read the code snippet above in plain English, you see that it calculates someone's age by subtracting the year of birth from the current year. Let's say your year of birth is 2013 and the current year is 2023, then you do the math:

$$2023 - 2013 = 10$$

The AgeCalculator function asks for two parameters/arguments from you: the year of birth and the current year. After doing the calculation, it gives a number as a result. Since the return type is an integer, this method will return a number. In this context, it returns someone's age after some calculations.

Now it's your turn. Decide what should be the return type for the following functions: Boolean or Integers. If you think it should be a boolean, write "bool". If you think the return type should be an integer, then write "int".

1. public _____ IsHeAvailable(string answer)

2. public _____ SubtractNumbers(int number1, int number2)

3. public _____ IsRequestSuccessful(int statusCode)

4. public _____ DivideNumbers(int number1, int number2)

5. public _____ IsTankFull(int weight)

So far, we've talked about three return types: void, boolean, and integer. To summarize, the void return type does not return anything, so we don't use the "return" keyword in it as we do in "boolean" and "integer" return types. Void methods perform tasks you request from them, but they don't return a value when you call them. On the other hand, boolean return type returns either true or false. Since there must be a boolean value return here, we use the "return" keyword in it. The latest one we learned is "integer". The integer return type returns a number. Like the Boolean type, it is returning a value to us, so we use the "return" keyword in it.

We will learn one more return type: "string". String methods return some string values. Since they are returning values, we also use the "return" keyword with string return type methods. Let's look at the example below:

```
public string FindTheCapitalOfACountry(string countryName)
{
    if (countryName.Equals("Turkiye"))
    {
        return "Ankara";
    }
    else if (countryName.Equals("United States of America"))
    {
        return "Washington D.C.";
    }
    else if (countryName.Equals("South Korea"))
    {
        return "Seoul";
    }
    else
    {
        return "Not found";
    }
}
```

The function above asks you to pass a country name as a parameter, and it returns the capital of the country you passed. The example above is not a completely finished example, but it gives you an idea of how we program functions like that. In the example, we programmed the function to look for certain string values like

"South Korea" and to return its capital. You teach it, and it gives you back what you taught. It's looking for an exact word match to give you the result.

You've learned a lot so far. We've introduced some new terms and symbols in this chapter. You might be thinking that you need to memorize all the curly braces or semi-colons you see in the examples, but you don't. That's not our goal. As you progress, everything will come together. The important thing is understanding the logic behind programming. As you've seen from the examples so far, we teach it or we can say we program it - and we get back what we taught and gave.

Now that we have covered some fundamentals of programming, including the purpose of functions and the different types of return values and access modifiers, you can start exploring more complex programming concepts. Remember, it's not about memorizing every single detail, but understanding the logic and principles behind them. As you continue on your programming journey, you'll start recognizing patterns and developing a deeper understanding of how different parts of code work together to create a functioning program.

Let's continue deepening our understanding of the overall structure. We have previously discussed the concept of arguments or parameters. Parameters are the data a function or method requires in order to perform its task. Consider the following example:

```
public string FindTheCapitalOfACountry(string countryName)
```

In the above example, countryName is a parameter of string type. This indicates that when calling the FindTheCapitalOfACountry method, you need to provide a country name. Without this parameter, the function wouldn't know the capital of which country you're seeking. Upon providing the country name, the function returns the corresponding capital.

Here's another example:

---

public int AgeCalculator(int yearOfBirth, int currentYear)

The AgeCalculator method requires two integer parameters: yearOfBirth and currentYear. Without these values, the function wouldn't be able to calculate an individual's age.

Parameters are crucial for directing the behavior of our methods and obtaining the desired output. Initially, we conceptualize the task we want our program to perform. Next, we devise a strategy or logic to achieve that task and translate it into code that the computer can understand.

Keep in mind that your objective here isn't to memorize the information shared; it's to understand the logic and the broader approach to programming and structuring your code. Programming is a field that is best learned through hands-on experience. Therefore, relax and strive to assimilate the concepts you've encountered thus far.

Now, let's discuss function names. So far, we've introduced several functions, including:

- SayHello
- PrintLaserPointerReservations
- IsAttending
- AgeCalculator
- FindTheCapitalOfACountry

Examining these function names, you might notice certain commonalities. Take your time and write them down.

_____

_____

_____

Firstly, the initial letter of each word is capitalized, with no spaces or symbols in between the words. This naming convention is known as "Camel Case". The name might seem odd, but picture a camel: the first thing you see is its head, akin to the capitalized first letter of a function name, followed by its humps, analogous to the capitalized letters that start each subsequent word.

Several other naming conventions exist, such as "Kebab Case" and "Snake Case", but in this book, we'll primarily use Camel Case. Familiarity with this naming convention should suffice for our purposes.

A further shared characteristic of these method names is that they all depict an action or a task. Since you program a method to execute certain operations, it's appropriate that your method name clearly articulates the action it performs. This contributes to the readability and understandability of your code, enhancing its quality and maintainability.

You might wonder why there's a need for clarity. After all, you might argue, you understand your code perfectly well. However, writing code is akin to writing an essay or paper - it should be clear enough for anyone who might work on the same project as you. Consider tech companies: they employ thousands of developers. To ensure that everyone is aligned, they establish and follow certain standards. Without such standards, understanding another's code could require a considerable time investment. Additionally, as your project expands, even you might lose track of every single detail in your own code. Therefore, it's always wise to make everything as clear as possible and meticulously document all functions.

Now, let's discuss curly braces "{}". As you might have noticed in all the code examples above, after declaring a function, we encapsulate our implementation within curly braces "{}". Think of curly braces as defining a chapter in a book. Whatever resides within these braces pertains solely to that specific function, reducing potential confusion or conflict with other methods. You could consider curly braces as separators, distinguishing a function from the other parts of the code implemented in a class.

We've now covered method declaration conventions and their meanings. Next, it's time to delve into the workings of a method.

At the beginning of this chapter, we explored some examples of void return type methods. To save you the effort of scrolling back, I've included it below:

```
public void SayHello()
{
    Console.WriteLine("Hello, My Friend!!!");
}
```

The "magic" happens within the curly braces. We first encounter "Console". Are you wondering what this "Console" is? It might be worthwhile to do a quick internet search.

"Console" is a class, and "WriteLine" is a method within the "Console" class. Yes, I know, I've just introduced a new term: "class". What's a class? You can think of it as analogous to a classroom at your school. There are different classrooms, and each one contains different students. Sometimes classrooms share the same teacher, like for music or PE, and sometimes they each have their own dedicated teacher.

In programming, we use classes to organize our code according to its purpose. This organization makes our code more readable and maintainable. Being organized is crucial; consider a library as an analogy. If you visit a library searching for a specific book but there's no order or classification, you'd have to scrutinize every single shelf to find your book. To avoid this chaos, librarians categorize books based on genre, type, year, and title, making it much easier for us to find what we need.

In our example, the "Console" class solely carries out actions related to the console. You might be wondering what a console is. Software developers typically use various tools to facilitate their programming tasks. For instance, Integrated Development Environments (IDEs) are software applications that help programmers develop software code efficiently. While working on their programs, developers can readily use the console to display outputs or monitor values being processed in the background. Essentially, you don't have to complete the entire program before seeing what's happening.

A team of developers recognized this need and developed a class of functions to execute console-related activities. We can thus easily use these pre-built functions to perform various actions.

Let's examine more examples:

```
public double SquareRoot(double a)
{
    return Math.Sqrt(a);
}
```

The method above uses a return type, "double", which we haven't delved into yet. You might recall our discussion about the integer return type, which returns numbers as a return value. "Double", however, can return numbers with decimal values like "4.5" or "9.7", whereas "Integer" can only return whole numbers. Consequently, using integer is sensible when calculating someone's age, but if you're handling accounting tasks or working with specific mathematical equations, you might need a type capable of working with decimals. In summary, "double" allows us to use numbers with decimal values.

In the example above, we invoke a class named "Math". Like the Console class, a group of developers came together and prepared this Math class for us to use. For instance, if you want to calculate the square root of any given number, you can simply call the "Sqrt()" method in the Math class. There's no need to write your own square root calculation method because one already exists.

You might be curious about the dot "." between the Math class and the Sqrt method. Using a dot "." essentially signifies that you want to access the methods or properties of a class. It helps you utilize the available fields or methods under it, akin to shopping from a programming class. When you employ a dot ".", you're essentially stating, "I want to shop from your dear programming class."

Furthermore, in all the examples you've seen so far, we've used a semicolon ";" at the end of some lines. The semicolon implies that a line of code is complete; it's ready to do what we've instructed it to. It has all the values, calls it needs, and we're ending that line of code. This is analogous to a period "." used when writing a paper or a letter. A period denotes the end of a sentence that includes all the points you wanted to convey to your readers. A semicolon ";" performs the same function in programming.

Let's consider another example from the Math class. Consider this exercise: Write an explanation about this method like how we explained the Math.Sqrt() one below. Pretend you're teaching this to a friend. So, try to simplify it as much as you can for someone unfamiliar with it.

```
public double Power(double a, double b)
{
    return Math.Pow(a, b);
}
```

The Power method: This method takes two parameters, a base "a" and an exponent "b", and returns the result of raising the base to the exponent.

_____

_____

_____

_____

Chapter 3 of our programming guide was designed to extend our foundational understanding of programming, delving into the particulars of how methods or functions operate in code. This chapter was instrumental in helping us grasp the role of return types, parameters, naming conventions, and other fundamental elements of a function.

In the beginning, we examined how parameters function as inputs to our methods. These parameters can be of various data types, like string or integer, and they guide the operation of the function. To illustrate, we used examples such as the FindTheCapitalOfACountry(string countryName) and AgeCalculator(int yearOfBirth, int currentYear) functions, emphasizing how the parameters shape the functionality and output of these methods. We recognized that when programming, we must first envisage what we want the software to accomplish and then strategize and implement a course of action that the computer can understand.

We then examined the naming conventions of functions, noticing a common pattern among them: CamelCase. This convention capitalizes the first letter of every word in a function name without spaces or special characters. This naming style not only maintains the code clean and legible but also signifies the purpose or action the method is intended to perform. A well-named function facilitates comprehension for other developers who might need to understand, maintain, or develop the code further.

Additionally, we explored the role of curly braces in encapsulating the logic within a function, similar to the way chapters in a book separate different sections. Anything within these braces belongs to that specific function and does not interfere with other code outside it.

Moreover, we delved into the practical usage of classes in organizing our code. Just like a school has different classes with various students, a program can have different classes containing distinct methods. We used the Console class as an example, explaining its role in outputting data to the console, and we also discussed the Math class that provides numerous helpful methods for mathematical operations.

The chapter culminated by introducing some common symbols in programming. The dot operator, which accesses methods or properties within a class, and the semicolon, which signifies the end of a code line, were explained using everyday examples for better understanding.

In summary, Chapter 3 effectively deepened our understanding of methods in programming. The concepts elucidated in this chapter, such as parameters, naming conventions, the role of braces, the importance of well-structured and well-named classes, and common programming symbols, are fundamental to writing good, maintainable code. As we progress through this book, these foundational principles will continue to play an integral role in our journey of mastering programming. Moving forward, we aim to build upon these basics, constantly reinforcing them through practice and application.

Fun Fact

The first gigabyte drive cost $40.000

In 1980, IBM unveiled the 3380, the world's first disk drive with a gigabyte capacity. It had the dimensions of a refrigerator, weighed 550 pounds, and had a price tag of $40,000.

Fun Fact Activity

Create a fun fact for year of 2060

Imagine you're in the year 2060 and think about what could be considered a "fun fact" during that time. Create your own fun fact for the year 2040! Include a title, content and drawing.

Fun Fact

EVENT PLANNING – SETTING THE STAGE

Scientists observe nature, conduct experiments, and collect data. Their aim is to decipher natural events and occurrences using the data they've amassed. Their explanations should be grounded in this collected data. The importance of data in this process is paramount, hence they pay considerable attention to storing it securely for future use or reassessment of their hypotheses.

Let's pause for a moment. Do you know what data means? You don't need to provide a dictionary-style definition, but consider what it means to you. Jot down your personal understanding of data below, based on your experiences or prior knowledge.

_____

_____

_____

Data comes in various forms: words, images, audio, or numbers. Think about how we can store these types of data. Outside the realm of computers, we record words on paper, which, when compiled, form larger entities such as books. Similarly, we print images and store them in photo albums. However, with the everyday use of computers and digital technology, our means of storing and utilizing data have transformed.

In Chapter 3, we discussed different return types. For instance, if our function returns a number as a result, we use an "integer" return type; if our method returns a word, we use a "string" return type. Similarly, the way we store data aligns with these types. Just as books store words, string variables hold string values, and integer variables store numerical values.

Variables can be thought of as containers. Each variable is designed to store a specific type of data. For instance, you wouldn't store sugar and milk in the same container. Every container has its own unique contents. You wouldn't look for your toys in the refrigerator. You have a designated toy box for them.

It's a useful analogy to think of data types as containers in programming. We can store numbers in an integer container or true/false statements in Boolean containers. We can modify what's inside a container as needed. Similar to how you might remove toys from your toy box, add new ones, or discard some, we can often make similar adjustments to the contents of programming containers.

Let's take a moment to acquaint ourselves with data types.

Characters & Strings

Char	String
'C'	"Hello"
'c'	"Ahmet"
'D'	"Anastasya"
'a'	"Sonya"

Integral Data Types

Short	Integer	Long
3	3	34592342345L
36	36	986686746343L
100	100	3454535345347L
32767	2147483647	5L

Floating Data Types

Float	Double
1.55f	2.23
100.01f	3.45
67.89f	22.78
1223.01f	100.01

Boolean Data Type

Boolean
TRUE
FALSE

Each data type has its own unique characteristics. Let's dive into more detail with the string data type.

String

A string data type stores string values. String values are represented within quotation marks (" "). Even if you see numbers or other symbols enclosed within these quotation marks, they are still considered string values. Think of a writer composing a sentence like "I'm 11 years old." In this case, we want to store the whole sentence, not just the numerical value.

Remember, a string value doesn't have to be meaningful or make logical sense. Whatever resides between those quotation marks is accepted as a string.

Some examples of string values:

"I love chocolate cake", "Sunny", "42 years old", "A", "True", "45"

You might wonder how "42" is a string value. It's considered a string value because it's enclosed in quotation marks. The same applies to "True" and "A".

Now that you understand what a string value is, the next step is learning how to store it. Just as you need paper to write on and store your writing, you need a container to save your string values. This allows you to retrieve it later, assign new values to it, or delete its content.

Let's examine how we store string values with the examples below:

```
string lastName = "Turkman";
string name = "Ahmet";
string countryName = "Turkiye";
string sisterName = "Anastasya";
```

What common features do you see in these examples? List three common aspects:

1. _____
2. _____
3. _____

The first commonality you likely noticed is that all of them start with the word "string". Indeed, we first declare the data type before creating a variable. Essentially, you're informing your computer that you're creating a string variable and will be saving a string value in it.

The second common aspect is that all the variables have names. We name our variables so we can call and use them when needed. Think of it like every person having a name. We use their name to call them or if we want to communicate something to them.

The third common feature is that all the string values are enclosed in quotation marks. As we mentioned earlier, a string value is declared within quotation marks.

Character/Char

Like strings, char values are stored within single quotation marks ("). However, unlike strings, only one single character can be placed between these quotation marks. If you need to store something longer, you'll have to use a string variable instead of char. When we declare a character data type, we use the abbreviation 'char'.

Let's examine some examples of char data types:

'A', 'c', 'Z', 'j', '1', '=', '@', '*', '#', ' ', '+', '-', '0'

As evident from the examples above, all are represented within single quotation marks. And it's not just English alphabets; numbers and symbols can also be used.

Now, let's see how we declare char values and store them.

char lastNameInitial = 'T';
char firstNameInitial = 'A';

```
char driverLicenseCode = 'H';
char countryCode= '1';
```

There are a few commonalities among these declarations. They all start with the "char" keyword, indicating the type of the data we'll be storing. Next, we define the variable name, which is used to store our char value. Whenever we need to use this char variable, we call it by the assigned name. Another shared feature is the use of single quotation marks (' '). This sets char apart from string; while string values are enclosed in double quotation marks, char values are enclosed in single quotation marks. Also, you'll have noticed that only one character is allowed between the single quotation marks. If you need to store something longer, you'll need a different variable type, not char.

Numeric Data Types

When working with numbers in programming, we store them in numeric data types. Although we've seen a few examples of these numeric values previously, we're going to delve deeper in this section. There are three main types of numeric data types:

- Integer types
- Floating-point types
- Decimal type.

We'll explore these numeric data types further in subsequent sections and gain a better understanding of them through some activities.

Integer Types

Primarily, we store whole numeric values in four different containers or data types:

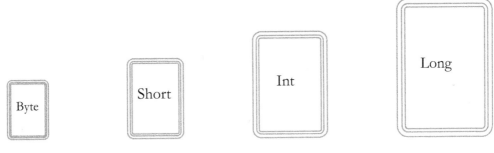

As illustrated above, these types vary in size, meaning each can hold a different maximum value. Think of these types like toy boxes. The "byte" toy box is the smallest, holding the fewest toys, while the "long" box is the largest, accommodating the most toys.

You might be wondering why we need differently sized 'boxes' in computing. The answer generally revolves around efficiency. For instance, imagine a classroom with 20 students. How many desks do you need? Most would reason that each student needs a desk, therefore, 20 should suffice. Others might suggest having a few spare desks. However, if you proposed 40 desks, the room would become overcrowded and less functional.

The same reasoning applies to data types in computing. We aim to maximize space by not allocating unnecessary resources. As physical space is limited in a classroom, so is a computer's memory. Consequently, we strive for maximum efficiency.

Now let's consider the size of these data types:

byte => 0 to 255

short => -32,768 to 32,767

int => -2,147,483,648 to 2,147,483,647

long => -9,223,372,036,854,775,808 to 9,223,372,036,854,775,807

These figures represent the maximum and minimum values storable in each corresponding data type. For instance, you can't store the number 256 in a byte type since the maximum is 255. However, you can store any number within the given limits in a larger type.

For example, you could store the number 5 in all four types of integer data types. You could place it in a byte, short, int, or long type. However, you couldn't store the number 500 in a byte type. If you think of it as a box, it exceeds the maximum capacity, necessitating a larger box.

Exercise time! Below are some empty boxes. Fill them with numeric values, considering the maximum size capacity mentioned earlier.

Byte	Short	Int	Long

Now, match the given values with the appropriate box, maximizing efficiency. This means you should assign values to the smallest possible containers. For example, there's no need to assign the number 12 to a 'long' container when you can fit it into a 'byte' container.

Values:

A. 256

B. 1

C. 32,768

D. 32,765

E. 5,000,000

F. 0

G. 2,147,483,648

H. 2,147,483,647

I. 4,000,000,000

J. -4,000,000,000

K. 255

L. 11,111

Byte	Short	Int	Long

Well done, these are easy to grasp. Now, let's learn how we declare and store integer values in programming. Storing integer values is similar to storing string or character values. First, we declare the data type, then we give a name to our variable, and finally, we assign the value we want.

For example:

byte age = 11;

short pocketMoney = 25;

int numberOfDays = 365;

long rainDropCount = 5555555555L;

long earthPopulation = 753553094L;

In the examples above, we began by stating the data type we wanted to store our data in. If you want to put a value into a 'byte' container, you declare a 'byte' variable and then give it a name. Once you've assigned your value, you conclude the statement with a semicolon ";". As you may remember from previous chapters, we use semicolons to end statements.

We also discussed the size of these types and went through the max and min size limits. Keep in mind, you can put smaller values into larger containers, like 'int' or 'long', but you cannot fit larger values into smaller containers.

When using 'long' type variables, we add the letter "L" or "l" at the end of the number to denote its type.

Floating Point Types

Floating data types include 'float' and 'double'. We use 'float' and 'double' to represent non-integer (fractional) numbers. There is one more data type used to represent fractions, but we will discuss that after floating point types.

The difference between 'float' and 'double' lies in their precision. 'Float' is 32 bits and has a precision of 7 digits, whereas 'double' is 64 bits and has a precision of 15-17 digits. If this seems overwhelming, think of it like 'integer' vs 'long' - 'double' has a larger capacity than 'float'.

64 bit

32 bit

Float   Double

Declaring floating point types is similar to integer types. Recall that 'long' type values end with the letter "L"; in the same way, 'float' type values end with the letter "f".

For example:

double bagWeight = 49.66;   float catWeight = 10.51f;

float carSpeed = 70.50f;   double dogWeight = 66.66;

float gumPrice = 1.50f;

Let's do some exercises. Create the following variables and assign values of your choice:

1. A 'float' type variable to store a candy bar's weight.

_____

2. A 'double' type to store a school bus's weight.

_____

3. A 'double' type to store an eagle's height.

_____

4. A 'float' type to store a worm's height.

_____

5. A 'float' type to store your age.

_____

You might be wondering when to use 'float' or 'double'. The choice depends on the size of the data you need. 'Float' type provides 7-digit precision, while 'double' type offers 15-17 digits of precision. Depending on your needs, you can choose either of these types. Keep in mind that you can always assign smaller values into larger data types, but you can't do the opposite - you can't assign large values into smaller data types. This is an important consideration when planning your application.

Decimal Type

The decimal type is the last numeric data type we'll cover. It's 128 bits and offers high precision of 28-29 digits. The decimal type uses more bits to represent a number with greater precision. This is especially important in finance. Although it uses 128 bits, its range is smaller than that of a double but larger than a float. All these extra bits are dedicated to providing more accurate information.

When declaring and initializing a decimal value, we add the letter "m" or "M" at the end of the value. As you may recall, for the "long" type we add the letter "l" or "L", and for "float" types we add the letter "f" or "F" at the end of the value. Now, let's learn how to declare and initialize a decimal value with the following examples:

decimal myPacketMoney = 10.25m;

decimal presidentsSalary = 500.63m;

decimal collegeSavings= 100.2515487m;

1. Declare and initialize a decimal type to represent your summer budget:

_____

2. Declare and initialize a decimal type to represent the total weight of the Earth:

_____

3. Declare and initialize a decimal type to represent your tooth fairy savings:

_____

4. Declare and initialize a decimal type to represent a sea turtle's speed:

_____

5. Declare and initialize a decimal type to represent a hamburger's price:

_____

Boolean Type

The boolean type can represent only true or false. It's used when we need to evaluate a condition that results in a binary outcome. A boolean is like a light switch; it's either on (true) or off (false).

For instance, when you ask your friend, "Are you hungry?" The answer is either yes (true) or no (false). So, in boolean, this can be represented as:

When naming a boolean variable, it's typical to phrase the variable name like a question, often starting with auxiliary verbs:

---

bool isRaining = false;

bool hasMoney = false;

bool isTvOn = true;

bool isHeHungry = true;

As you can see in the examples above, they are all phrased as questions, hence they can be answered as either yes (true) or no (false).

Let's declare and initialize the following boolean type examples:

1. You want to determine if your friend is happy:

_____

2. You want to check attendance for a birthday party:

_____

3. You want to know if your friends have pets:

_____

4. You want to know if your parents like football:

_____

5. You want to know if you're taller than 5 feet:

_____

Chapter 4 has provided an in-depth understanding of the various types of variables in programming. It is in this chapter that we've delved into the specifics of data types, demystifying the difference between them, understanding how to declare and initialize them, and learning when and why we would use each one. This new knowledge will be essential in your journey through programming, allowing you to be adaptable and resourceful as you develop your own code.

We began the chapter by understanding that variables act as containers or boxes in a computer's memory, each with its unique capacity and function. This concept is foundational in understanding how data is stored and manipulated within a program.

As we looked at string variables, we learned that they are used to store text, including words or sentences. String variables are versatile and can be used to store everything from user input to error messages. On the other hand, we also discussed character variables, which are used to store single letters or characters. This distinction is crucial in understanding the flexibility and limitations of textual data storage in programming.

The chapter then moved to a discussion about boolean variables, which are used to store true or false values. These are often used to control program flow or check conditions. Boolean variables are like light switches, either on or off, true or false. This binary state is the core of many decision-making processes within a program.

Lastly, we delved into numeric data types, which include integer, floating-point, and decimal types. We learned that integer types are used to store whole numbers. For numbers with decimal points, floating-point types (double and float) and decimal types come into play. We noted that the type of numeric variable to be used is determined by the level of precision needed. Double variables are the most commonly used due to their balance of precision and storage size.

This chapter has provided an expansive view of the landscape of data types. From string to boolean, integer to decimal, the choice of which type to use is guided by the requirements of our program, the precision needed, and the memory available. Understanding these different variables, their characteristics, and their proper application, equips us with the necessary tools to be effective and efficient programmers.

As we conclude this chapter, it's essential to recognize the importance of these fundamental concepts. The knowledge of these variable types is not just about the specific applications; it's also about understanding the broader context of how data is represented and manipulated in a program. Each variable type has its role, and understanding these roles allows us to create programs that are efficient, accurate, and robust.

As we move forward, remember that these are your tools in the vast world of programming. They are here to assist you in crafting your code, to create programs that can do everything from solving complex mathematical problems to providing interactive user experiences. Keep practicing, keep exploring, and keep coding!

Fun Fact

MyDoom is the Most Expensive Computer Virus in History

The Mydoom virus, true to its foreboding name, rapidly proliferated through emails in January 2004. It's estimated that the virus was responsible for generating 16 to 25 percent of all emails sent that year.

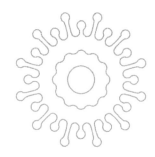

Fun Fact Activity

Create a fun fact for year of 2100

Imagine you're in the year 2100 and think about what could be considered a "fun fact" during that time. Create your own fun fact for the year 2040! Include a title, content and drawing.

Fun Fact

5

EVENT EXECUTION – CONDUCTING THE SYMPHONY

Congrats, young coders! You've learned so much already about programming fundamentals. Now, if anyone asks you about variables or functions, you're all set to explain. But, you might be wondering, "how does everything work together?" Knowing individual parts is good, but it's like having a bunch of Lego blocks and not knowing how to connect them. That's why this chapter is super important. Here, we'll learn how to put variables, functions, and classes together, like building an amazing Lego structure. This will make you ready for some super cool advanced topics. Let's get started!

Task 1:

Let's imagine your school is planning a big end-of-year dinner for all students and their parents. The teachers have asked for volunteers to help organize the event, and you, being a helpful superstar, have said, "yes!" Here are some things you'll need to organize:

- The number of people coming to the dinner.
- The names of all participants.
- The dinner selection for each person. They can choose from:
    - Vegetarian
    - Vegan
    - Beef
- Printing out the participants' names.
- Making name tags for everyone.
- Figuring out the seating arrangements.
- Preparing a music playlist and organizing a music player.

Wow, that sounds like a lot, but don't worry! Let's break it down and come up with a step-by-step plan to make this a night everyone will remember. Being an event planner is a big responsibility, but with some good planning, you can make it super fun!

Use the space below to write down your plan. Remember, good planning is the key to a successful event!

_____

_____

_____

_____

_____

_____

_____

_____

Awesome! Now let's think about how a programmer might approach this task.

A programmer would first look for common themes that can be grouped together. Just like when you're organizing your toys or books, you'd want all your Legos or comic books together, right? Similarly, in coding, it's super important to keep things organized.

Imagine a library with no order - it'd be impossible to find your favorite book! To avoid that chaos, we need classes in our code.

We'll need a class that handles the names of participants and their dinner choices. But why do we need classes? Well, classes are like the signs in a library. They specialize in a particular area. So if you're looking for a book on dinosaurs, you know exactly where to go. Similarly, classes in programming help keep our code neat, organized, and easy to understand. More on that soon!

Let's create a class called "Participant" to handle the participant's name and dinner selection. Here's how we do it in code:

```
using System;
using System.Collections.Generic;

public class Participant
{
    public string Name { get; set; }
    public DinnerOption DinnerSelection { get; set; }

    public Participant(string name, DinnerOption dinnerSelection)
```

```
    {
        Name = name;
        DinnerSelection = dinnerSelection;
    }
}
```

Alright, let's untangle this coding knot together. We've made a class named "Participant". It's like a personal folder for each participant. Inside this folder, we're storing two pieces of information: the participant's name and their dinner choice.

The 'public' before the class name means anyone can access this class, like an open library. 'Using' at the top helps us borrow some handy tools from the 'System' library.

You'll see 'get' and 'set' inside curly braces. Without going into too many details, these let us give a value to the Name and DinnerSelection and also use those values elsewhere in our code.

Now, you might wonder about the DinnerSelection variable. It's not a string or an integer. Surprise! It's a custom type variable that we've created. Here's how we've done it:

```
public enum DinnerOption
{
    Vegetarian,
    Vegan,
    Beef
}
```

This is called an 'enum' or enumerator. It's a list of values that we create. For our dinner, we've listed three options: Vegetarian, Vegan, and Beef. It's like a special menu with only three choices.

Lastly, we've used something called a 'constructor' in our Participant class. You can think of it as a special method that helps set up our class with the right information. When you make a new 'Participant', you must provide a name and their dinner selection.

Don't worry if it's a bit much! We'll delve deeper into these exciting topics in our future books. For now, remember that coding is like building with Legos. Each piece has a purpose and they all connect to create something awesome!

Next, we need to manage the seating arrangements for our dinner. To do this, we're going to create a new class called "Table".

```
public class Table
{
    public List<Participant> Participants { get; set; }

    public Table()
    {
        Participants = new List<Participant>();
    }

    public void AddParticipant(Participant participant)
    {
        Participants.Add(participant);
```

```
    }
  }
```

In this class, we've got a list of participants. A list is like a line at the ice-cream store. It's a way to organize lots of things, or in our case, participants, in a specific order.

```
public List<Participant> Participants { get; set; }
```

Here's how it works: 'public' means anyone can access our list. 'List' is the tool we're using to store our data. 'Participant' is the type of data we're storing - kind of like declaring "this line is for people who want ice cream, not sandwiches". And 'Participants' is the name of our list.

Did you notice the 's' at the end of 'Participants'? This is a small hint to tell us that we're dealing with a list that contains multiple 'Participant' data.

So, with our 'Table' class, we've created a way to manage a list of participants for our dinner. It's like a digital seating chart!

Next on our list is creating a playlist for our dinner party. To do this, we're going to create a new class called "MusicPlayer". Just like before, we'll need a list since a playlist has more than one song. This time, our list will store song names, which are strings. Let's make this list and name it "Playlist".

```
public List<string> Playlist { get; set; }
```

We'll also set up a constructor in this class to start our playlist. But that's not all. Our "MusicPlayer" class is going to have two functions: one for adding songs to our playlist, and one for playing the music.

```
public class MusicPlayer
{
    public List<string> Playlist { get; set; }

    public MusicPlayer()
    {
        Playlist = new List<string>();
    }

    public void AddSong(string song)
    {
        Playlist.Add(song);
    }

    public void Play()
    {
        Console.WriteLine("Playing music...");
    }
}
```

Here's a fun fact: when we want to add songs to our playlist, we call a special method of our "Playlist" list called "Add". This is like telling our list, "Hey, we've got a new song to add to the party!".

Remember, there are many other things we can do with lists, but for now, we'll just focus on adding items with the "Add" method. Think of it as a sneak peek into the exciting world of programming lists!

So far, we've created three classes and an enumerator for meal options. But how do we make all these parts work together like a well-rehearsed orchestra? That's where our next class comes in!

We're going to create a new class called "SchoolEvent". This class will be like our orchestra conductor, coordinating everything so our event runs smoothly.

In our "SchoolEvent" class, we're going to call on the "Participant" class to get our list of participants, the "Table" class to organize our seating arrangements, and the "MusicPlayer" class to create our playlist.

First, let's set up our constructor so that it starts these variables when our "SchoolEvent" class begins:

```
public SchoolEvent()
{
    Participants = new List<Participant>();
    Tables = new List<Table>();
    MusicPlayer = new MusicPlayer();
}
```

Now, let's create our first method in this class to add participants to our

"Participants" list:

```
public void AddParticipant(Participant participant)
{
    Participants.Add(participant);
}
```

Notice that our method takes one argument, a participant, which is an instance of our custom "Participant" class. This means that to add a participant to the list, you have to pass the participant's name and dinner selection, as we configured in the constructor of the "Participant" class. It's like giving a ticket to each participant to join our fun-filled school event!

Now, it's time for us to arrange the tables! We're going to create a function called "ArrangeTables", which will decide how many participants can sit at each table. Here's how it works:

```
public void ArrangeTables(int participantsPerTable)
{
        int tableCount = (int)Math.Ceiling((double)Participants.Count / participantsPerTable);

    for (int i = 0; i < tableCount; i++)
    {
        Tables.Add(new Table());
```

```
    }

    for (int i = 0; i < Participants.Count; i++)
    {
        int tableIndex = i % tableCount;
        Tables[tableIndex].AddParticipant(Participants[i]);
    }
}
```

First, the function figures out how many tables we'll need by dividing the total number of participants by the number of participants we want at each table. We use Math.Ceiling to round up to the next whole number to make sure everyone gets a seat, even if it means the last table isn't completely full.

Next, the function creates the right number of Table objects and adds them to our list of Tables.

Lastly, it assigns each participant to a table. The function cycles through the list of tables, making sure each table gets a participant before moving on to the next round of assignments. This is done using a 'for loop', a programming concept that allows us to repeat a piece of code a certain number of times.

Imagine we have 10 participants, and we want no more than 3 participants at each table. Our function will make 4 tables (because 10 divided by 3 is about 3.33, and we round that up). Then, it assigns participants to the tables in this order:

Participant 1 ➡ Table 1,

Participant 2 ➡ Table 2,

Participant 3 ➡ Table 3,

Participant 4 Table 4,

Participant 5 Table 1,

... and so on.

This way, the tables fill up evenly. If there are any extra seats, they'll be at the last few tables. We've made sure everyone has a seat, and no table is overcrowded!

Next up, we're going to print out the participant names. However, when we say "print," we mean writing each participant's name on the console, not printing on paper. Here's the function for it:

```
public void PrintParticipantNames()
{
    Console.WriteLine("Participant Names:");
    foreach (Participant participant in Participants)
    {
        Console.WriteLine(participant.Name);
    }
}
```

To write each participant's name that's stored in our Participants list, we use a foreach loop. This type of loop is quite handy when we don't need to keep track of indices like in the for loop. It simplifies the process by directly dealing with the elements of the list.

In this foreach loop, we create an object of the Participant class and assign values from our Participants list one at a time. This allows us to print the participant names one by one instead of all together.

Now, let's look at another function, PrepareNameTags. Try to figure out what it does and how it works by comparing it with the PrintParticipantsNames function we just discussed.

```
public void PrepareNameTags()
{
    Console.WriteLine("Preparing Name Tags...");
    foreach (Participant participant in Participants)
    {
        Console.WriteLine($"Name tag for {participant.Name}");
    }
}
```

Can you write down what this function does and how it achieves its goal?

_____

_____

_____

_____

_____

We've now finished organizing our classes and methods for managing this event. Let's look at how we will use all the code we've prepared. Specifically, we'll examine our Main function that calls all the functions we've defined. The Main function is a crucial part of any program as it orchestrates the execution of all the code.

Here's how it looks:

```
public class Program
{
    public static void Main(string[] args)
    {
        SchoolEvent schoolEvent = new SchoolEvent();

        // Add participants
        schoolEvent.AddParticipant(new Participant("John Doe",
        DinnerOption.Vegetarian));
        schoolEvent.AddParticipant(new Participant("Jane Smith",
        DinnerOption.Beef));

        // Print participant names
        schoolEvent.PrintParticipantNames();

        // Prepare name tags
        schoolEvent.PrepareNameTags();

        // Arrange tables
        schoolEvent.ArrangeTables(4);

        // Add music to the playlist
        schoolEvent.MusicPlayer.AddSong("Happy");
        schoolEvent.MusicPlayer.AddSong("Uptown Funk");
```

```
    // Play music
    schoolEvent.MusicPlayer.Play();
  }
}
```

The first thing we do is create an instance of the SchoolEvent class, which encompasses all the methods and properties related to our event organization. This is done with the line: SchoolEvent schoolEvent = new SchoolEvent();.

Then, we add participants to our event by invoking the AddParticipant method of our SchoolEvent instance and passing in a new Participant object.

Following that, we call the PrintParticipantNames method to output the names of all the event's participants to the console.

Now, let's see if you can describe   what the following function does:

```
schoolEvent.PrepareNameTags();
```

_____

_____

_____

_____

Subsequently, we call the ArrangeTables method of the SchoolEvent class, which organizes the seating arrangements for the event. We pass 4 as an argument, indicating that each table should seat 4 participants: schoolEvent.ArrangeTables(4);.

Lastly, we use the MusicPlayer property of the SchoolEvent class to manage the event's music. We call the AddSong method to add songs to the playlist, and then Play method to start the music:

```
// Add music to the playlist
schoolEvent.MusicPlayer.AddSong("Happy");
schoolEvent.MusicPlayer.AddSong("Uptown Funk");

// Play music
schoolEvent.MusicPlayer.Play();
```

In Chapter 5, we ventured into the realm of programming by simulating the organization of a school event. Leveraging principles of Object-Oriented Programming (OOP), we constructed various components using C# language constructs, including classes, properties, methods, and enumerators. We gained insights into encapsulation by defining distinct classes like Participant, Table, and MusicPlayer, each endowed with its own properties and methods. Furthermore, we navigated through the interactions between these classes within the context of the SchoolEvent class, which functioned as the conductor of our virtual event.

In the process, we not only unveiled the basic principles of programming but also underscored the crucial role of problem-solving, logical reasoning, and strategic organization in the sphere of software development. We planned, coded, and implemented each part of our program, thus experiencing the compelling capacity of programming firsthand.

Upon completion of this chapter, congratulations are in order! You have adeptly applied programming concepts to execute a school event, thereby gaining a pragmatic understanding of how programmers navigate problem-solving. This immersive journey has shed light on the iterative and innovative essence of programming. Always remember that understanding the underlying concepts and regular practice outweigh the simple act of reaching the end of a chapter or book. Therefore, reflect upon the lessons imparted, revisit the exercises, and constantly strive to enhance your understanding and proficiency.

In the grand scheme of things, programming is a lifelong journey, characterized by continual learning and growth. The pillars of success in this field are self-discipline and persistent hard work. The knowledge you've garnered thus far lays a robust foundation for your future endeavors, but bear in mind that the universe of programming is vast and ever-evolving. Therefore, challenge yourself persistently, push your boundaries, and make a consistent effort to enrich your repository of knowledge each day. This approach will ensure that you stay ahead in this dynamic field and continue to harness the power of programming to build innovative solutions.

Fun Fact Activity
Create a fun fact for year of 2500

Imagine you're in the year 2500 and think about what could be considered a "fun fact" during that time. Create your own fun fact for the year 2040! Include a title, content and drawing.

Fun Fact

6

AUTHOR'S MESSAGE

Bravo on completing this foundational journey into the world of programming! This book was designed to equip you with basic programming concepts and help you develop the mindset of a software developer. Now, with a holistic picture of programming, you have taken your first big step into this vast, exciting field.

Remember, the process of learning programming is not linear but rather an ongoing, iterative endeavor. You'll face challenges, experience successes, and sometimes even taste failures - all of these are integral parts of the journey. Embrace them, learn from them, and grow.

As you progress, remember to continuously reassess your knowledge. The aim is not to finish books but to internalize their lessons. Don't compare your progress with others - this is your journey, and it's your development that matters.

When you feel ready to deepen your programming skills further, we have more advanced books awaiting you. Each one is designed to build upon the knowledge you've gained, introducing new concepts, languages, and applications of programming.

Thank you for choosing our book as your stepping stone into the programming universe. We hope that this has been an enriching and empowering journey for you, and we look forward to supporting your future learning endeavors.

Until we meet again in the next book, happy coding!

Congratulations

ABOUT THE AUTHOR

Burak Turkman is a seasoned .NET developer and a passionate educator. Beginning his professional journey as a specialist in gifted education, he focused his studies on creativity and giftedness, pioneering the development of computerized creativity assessments. With his roots firmly planted in education, Burak held teaching positions at renowned institutions, such as Istanbul University and the University of Nebraska - Lincoln.

In his quest to impart knowledge, he provided professional development training to fellow educators, fostering a culture of continuous learning and growth. Burak holds a Ph.D. in Educational Psychology.

However, what truly kindles his enthusiasm is the world of programming. He relishes not just the act of coding but also the joy of teaching it. By blending his profound knowledge of education with his expertise in .NET development, Burak seeks to make programming an accessible and enjoyable experience for young learners. In his book, he aims to ignite a passion for coding among early coders who are older than 10, encouraging them to innovate, create, and discover the boundless possibilities of programming.

Notes

Notes

www.ingramcontent.com/pod-product-compliance
Lightning Source LLC
LaVergne TN
LVHW081347050326
832903LV00024B/1357